W9-ACJ-585

🕮 READERS

Level 2

Dinosaur Dinners
Fire Fighter!
Bugs! Bugs! Bugs!
Slinky, Scaly Snakes!
Animal Hospital
The Little Ballerina
Munching, Crunching, Sniffing,
  and Snooping
The Secret Life of Trees
Winking, Blinking, Wiggling,
  and Waggling
Astronaut: Living in Space

Twisters!
Holiday! Celebration Days
  around the World
The Story of Pocahontas
Horse Show
Survivors: The Night the Titanic Sank
Eruption! The Story of Volcanoes
The Story of Columbus
Journey of a Humpback Whale
Amazing Buildings
LEGO: Castle Under Attack!
LEGO: Rocket Rescue

Level 3

Spacebusters
Beastly Tales
Shark Attack!
Titanic
Invaders from Outer Space
Movie Magic
Plants Bite Back!
Time Traveler
Bermuda Triangle
Tiger Tales
Aladdin
Heidi
Zeppelin: The Age of the Airship
Spies
Terror on the Amazon

Disasters at Sea
The Story of Anne Frank
Abraham Lincoln: Lawyer, Leader,
  Legend
George Washington: Soldier, Hero,
  President
Extreme Sports
Spiders' Secrets
LEGO: Mission to the Arctic
NFL: Troy Aikman
NFL: Super Bowl Heroes
NFL: Peyton Manning
MLB: Home Run Heroes: Big Mac,
  Sammy, and Junior
MLB: Roberto Clemente

Level 4

Days of the Knights
Volcanoes and Other Natural Disasters
Secrets of the Mummies
Pirates!
Horse Heroes
Trojan Horse
Micromonsters
Going for Gold!
Extreme Machines
Flying Ace: The Story of Amelia Earhart
Robin Hood
Black Beauty
Free at Last! The Story of
  Martin Luther King, Jr.
Joan of Arc
Spooky Spinechillers
Welcome to The Globe! The
  Story of Shakespeare's Theater
Antarctic Adventure
Space Station
Atlantis
Dinosaur Detectives

Danger on the Mountain: Scaling
  the World's Highest Peaks
Crime Busters
The Story of Muhammad Ali
LEGO: Race for Survival
NFL: NFL's Greatest Upsets
NFL: Terrell Davis
NFL: Rambling Running Backs
WCW: Going for Goldberg
WCW: Feel the Sting!
WCW: Fit for the Title
WCW: Finishing Moves
MLB: Strikeout Kings
MLB: Super Shortstops: Jeter,
  Nomar, and A-Rod
The Story of the X-Men: How it
  all Began
Creating the X-Men: How Comic
  Books Come to Life
Spider-Man's Amazing Powers
The Story of Spider-Man

A Note to Parents

DK READERS is a compelling program for beginning readers, designed in conjunction with leading literacy experts, including Dr. Linda Gambrell, Director of the School of Education at Clemson University. Dr. Gambrell has served on the Board of Directors of the International Reading Association and as President of the National Reading Conference.

Beautiful illustrations and superb full-color photographs combine with engaging, easy-to-read stories to offer a fresh approach to each subject in the series. Each DK READER is guaranteed to capture a child's interest while developing his or her reading skills, general knowledge, and love of reading.

The four levels of DK READERS are aimed at different reading abilities, enabling you to choose the books that are exactly right for your child:

Level 1 – Beginning to read
Level 2 – Beginning to read alone
Level 3 – Reading alone
Level 4 – Proficient readers

The "normal" age at which a child begins to read can be anywhere from three to eight years old, so these levels are only a general guideline.

No matter which level you select, you can be sure that you are helping your child learn to read, then read to learn!

DK

LONDON, NEW YORK, DELHI, PARIS,
MUNICH AND MELBOURNE

Editor Alastair Dougall
Senior Art Editor Nick Avery
US Editor Beth Hester
Production Nicola Torode
Picture Researcher Carolyn Clerkin
Marvel Consultant Seth Lehman

Reading Consultant
Linda Gambrell, Ph.D.

First American Edition, 2003
03 04 05 06 07 10 9 8 7 6 5 4 3 2 1
Published in the United States by DK Publishing, Inc.
375 Hudson Street, New York, New York 10014

Copyright © 2003 Dorling Kindersley Limited, London

Published in Great Britain by Dorling Kindersley Limited.

Library of Congress Cataloging-in-Publication Data

Teitelbaum, Michael.
  The story of the Incredible Hulk / written by Michael Teitelbaum.--
1st American ed.
    p. cm.
The Incredible Hulk was created by writer Stan Lee and artist Jack Kirby.
Includes index.
  ISBN 0-7894-9544-9 (hardcover) -- ISBN 0-7894-9262-8 (pbk.)
  1. Hulk (Comic strip)--Juvenile literature. 2. Incredible Hulk
(Fictitious character)--Juvenile literature. I. Title.
  PN6728.H8 T457 2003
  741.5'973--dc21

                                             2002154179

Color reproduction by Media Development and Printing Ltd., England.
Printed and bound in China by L Rex Printing Co., Ltd.

The publisher thanks the following for their kind permission
to reproduce their photographs:
c=center; t=top; b=bottom; l=left; r=right

5: Hulton Archive/Getty Images tr; 6: Hulton Archive/Getty
Images/Keystone collection tl; MPI collection bc; 7: Hulton Archive/Getty
Images/American Stock crb; Popperfoto t; 8: Science Photo
Library/Alexander Tsiaras cl; 9: Science Photo Library/Biophoto
Associates tr; 10: Hulton Archive/Getty Images/Fox Photos tl;
11: Science Photo Library/Dr Jeremy Burgess br; 12: Rex Features/Sipa
Press cl; 13: Science Photo Library/Alexander Tsiaras tr;
14: Kobal Collection/Universal tl; 21: Getty Images/Jim Naughten tr;
33: Kate Howey & Elgan Loane, Kentree Ltd, Ireland br;
37: Corbis/D. Robert & Lorri Franz tr; 43: Corbis/Macduff Everton cr.

All other images © Dorling Kindersley.
For further information see: www.dkimages.com

MARVEL, Hulk and all related comic characters used: TM & © 2003 Marvel
Characters, Inc. All rights reserved. www.marvel.com.
This book is produced under license from Marvel Characters, Inc.

see our complete product line at
www.dk.com

Contents

DK READERS

PROFICIENT **4** READERS

THE STORY OF

THE INCREDIBLE HULK

Written by Michael Teitelbaum

DK Publishing

Man or monster?

In May 1962, a new character burst onto the pages of Marvel Comics. The Incredible Hulk was the creation of writer Stan Lee and artist Jack Kirby. This angry beast became the star of Marvel's second new series in what became known as the "Marvel Age" of comics. Seven feet tall and rippling with muscles from head to toe, the Incredible Hulk was a monstrous creature of enormous strength and uncontrollable rage. Unlike most comic characters, Hulk was not clearly a hero or a villain.

Green Hulk, as drawn by Jack "King" Kirby in the early 1960s. Unlike conventional super heroes, Hulk does not wear a special outfit.

Color change
Everyone knows the Incredible Hulk is green, right? Believe it or not, in his first appearance (Incredible Hulk #1) the big brute was gray! However, the printer had trouble with the gray color, and so in the next issue, the green Hulk was born.

Readers discovered how scientist Dr. Bruce Banner was caught in a blast of gamma radiation from a new kind of bomb. From then on, he would transform from his usual frail human form into the huge, brutish Hulk whenever he became angry.

Lee and Kirby got their inspiration from great literature. Robert Louis Stevenson's *The Strange Case of Dr. Jekyll and Mr. Hyde* tells the story of a scientist who changes back and forth into a rampaging beast. *Frankenstein* by Mary Shelley is about a monster that is feared by all, but is not truly evil.

The monster
The hideous Mr. Hyde and Frankenstein's monster have been scaring movie audiences stiff for decades. The first movie featuring Hyde dates back to 1921. The first Frankenstein film was made in 1931.

Hero team
The Fantastic Four kicked off the Marvel Age in 1961. The comic focused on the personalities of a team of super heroes as well as their battles.

Stockpiles
Both the
United States
and the Soviet
Union had
many nuclear
weapons at
their disposal
during the Cold
War.

World leaders
U.S. President
John F.
Kennedy (on
left) and Soviet
Chairman
Nikita
Khrushchev
were the
leaders of their
respective
nations at the
height of the
Cold War.

Cold War anxieties

In many ways, the Incredible
Hulk was a product of the
times in which he was created.
The concept of a character born of
an accident involving radioactivity
reflected what was happening in the
real world during that period of
history. Fear of nuclear weapons
and deadly radiation was an
everyday reality.

By 1962, the United States and a
group of countries including Russia,
collectively called the Soviet Union,
were involved in what became
known as "The Cold War."

Although these two great powers were never actually involved in a real war, the threat of such a destructive conflict created anxiety around the world.

These worries were reflected in the culture of the times. Many science-fiction movies showed invading aliens armed with radioactive weapons.

In Marvel Comics, Peter Parker was bitten by a radioactive spider and became Spider-Man. Bruce Banner, caught in the explosion of a radioactive weapon, transformed into the Incredible Hulk.

Cuban missile crisis
In 1962, the Soviet Union tried to set up a missile base in Cuba. This almost led to nuclear war with the U.S.

Duck & cover
In the 1950s, U.S. schools held bomb drills to show children what to do in case of a nuclear attack.

Meet Bruce Banner

Research
Many important scientific discoveries come out of the hard work of scientific researchers. Although their names usually remain unknown, their dedication has helped to improve life for everyone.

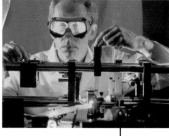

A scientist hard at work in the laboratory.

Dr. Robert Bruce Banner was a brilliant scientist. His specialty was nuclear physics. As a boy, Banner was extremely intelligent, yet shy and withdrawn. His father, Brian, was also an atomic scientist. But Brian was an angry man, who constantly yelled at young Bruce and his mother. Eventually, Brian went insane and was placed into a mental hospital.

This greatly affected Bruce who became even more timid, often feeling powerless. As an adult, Bruce's genius was recognized by the United States government. He was put to work at the U.S. Defense Department's nuclear research facility at Desert Base, New Mexico. There, he began research into a project that he hoped would make his dreams of power come true.

Little did he know that his experiments would lead to an event that would change his life forever.

Banner's work in the research facility led him to harness the awesome power of gamma radiation. He created a new type of weapon—the gamma bomb, also known as the "G-bomb."

DANGER RADIOACTIVE MATERIAL

Incredible energy
Energy given off by the nucleus of the atoms of certain elements is called radioactivity. This intense energy is used in medical tests and treatments, and as a source of power, as well as in destructive weapons.

Scientist
Brilliant but shy, Dr. Bruce Banner found working in a laboratory, hidden away from the world, was the perfect job for him.

The bomb
Nuclear bombs were invented in the 1940s and became the ultimate weapons of war. Today several nations possess these deadly weapons.

A dangerous test

The day to test Dr. Banner's powerful G-bomb finally arrived. The test was set up in an empty expanse of desert. Dr. Banner watched from a nearby bunker where he would be protected from the bomb's deadly radiation when it exploded.

"A few more seconds and we'll know whether or not we have succeeded," Banner said to his fellow scientists.

"I still say you should have shared the secret of your gamma bomb with the rest of us," commented a scientist named Igor. Dr. Banner didn't know that Igor was a Soviet spy, who had managed to infiltrate the project.

Before Banner could reply, General "Thunderbolt" Ross burst into the room. "What's the delay, Banner?" he blustered.

"Are you going to test that bomb or not?" shouted General Ross. He disliked Banner because he felt he was too cautious.

Banner turned to the control panel. At last, the moment of truth was at hand. "I've started the final countdown," he announced. Then, picking up a pair of binoculars, he peered out the bunker's window.

"Wait!" he shouted in alarm. "There's someone driving out into the test area!"

Unaware
Rick Jones had no idea that a bomb was about to explode when he took a dare and drove onto the test site.

Nuclear tests
Before nuclear bombs were used in war, they were tested on remote islands. They exploded, releasing huge radioactive clouds into the air.

A daring rescue

Banner watched in horror as a teenage boy drove straight towards the gamma bomb. "You've got to stop the countdown, Igor," he demanded. "I'm going to get that boy out of there."

"Sure," Igor replied, a devious plan forming in his mind. If Banner would not share the secret of the G-bomb with him, he would make sure that Banner perished in the explosion.

Dashing from the bunker, Banner quickly reached the boy in the car.

"You have to get out of here, now!" Banner shouted.

"My friends dared me to sneak past the guards and drive out here," the boy explained.

"You fool!" Banner cried, pulling the boy from the car, and shoving him into a nearby trench.

Back in the bunker, Igor did not try to stop the countdown and it reached zero.

KA-THOOM!

Before Bruce Banner managed to get into the protective trench, the gamma bomb detonated and he was bathed in the full force of its mysterious gamma radiation!

Protection
Scientists that work with radioactive material wear special protective suits that prevent the harmful radiation from touching their skin or penetrating their bodies.

Selfless
Bruce Banner made sure that Rick Jones was safely in the protective trench before the G-bomb went off. Unfortunately, Banner did not have time to get into the trench himself.

Night creatures
At first, the Hulk part of Bruce Banner only came out at night. Other "creatures of the night" from literature and movies include vampires, like Dracula.

Bats
Nature is also filled with creatures who sleep during the day and hunt for food at night. Perhaps the best known is the bat.

A transformation

When Banner awakened hours later, he found himself in a doctor's office. Standing beside him was the young man whose life he had saved.

"How did I get here?" Banner asked, still in shock.

"I brought you here," said the teenager. "My name is Rick Jones. It was the least I could do since you risked your life to save me."

"Banner, it's a miracle you're alive," explained the doctor. "You absorbed the full impact of the gamma rays."

As Banner rested, Rick Jones stayed right by his side. When the sun went down that night, Banner underwent an astounding change.

Rick Jones looked on in stunned amazement as Bruce Banner grew to twice his normal size. His skin turned a vivid shade of green.

When the transformation was complete, Bruce Banner had disappeared and in his place stood THE INCREDIBLE HULK!

Banner had become a huge, angry creature!

Coming apart
When Bruce Banner transforms into the Hulk, his body increases in size so dramatically that his clothes shred to bits.

Transformed
Over the years, Banner never got used to the amazing transformation that changed him into the Hulk. It always made him feel dizzy and disoriented.

Hulk mad!

Enraged, the Hulk rushed from the nuclear facility. General Ross sent out a squad of soldiers to stop the creature, who appeared to be a mindless, destructive animal.

Nicknames
Over the years the Hulk has acquired many nicknames including: The Green-Skinned Goliath, Jade-Jaws, The Emerald Behemoth, and Ol' Greenskin.

Changes
As time went by, Banner's transformation into the Hulk and back again stopped coinciding with the rising and setting of the sun. Instead, the change took place when Banner got angry.

"Leave me alone!" Hulk shouted, as he easily crushed a jeep with his powerful fists, causing soldiers to run for safety.

"Let's get away from that—that… Hulk!" cried one of the fleeing soldiers. And so the monster gained a name.

Rick Jones remained loyal to the man who had saved his life. In the morning, when the sun finally came up, the Hulk once again became Bruce Banner. Jones explained what had happened to him.

"It's over," Banner said, clutching his aching head. "The nightmare is over." But he was wrong. Each night Dr. Bruce Banner transformed once again.

And so, the mountain of muscle known as the Hulk was born, and fans instantly took to the most unusual character ever to grace the pages of a comic book!

Crafty
When he first burst onto the comic book scene, the Hulk was portrayed as crafty, mean, and filled with evil intentions.

Jeeps
Tough, rugged army jeeps are the main mode of ground transportation for military personnel. These four-wheel drive vehicles can easily handle rough terrain—even mountains!

Reluctant hero
Unlike most super-heroes who have been given amazing abilities, Bruce Banner hates his alter ego. It is not a source of pride or heroism. He lives his life in constant fear of changing into the Hulk.

Hero or villain?

Part of the Hulk's great appeal has always been the fact that he is not clearly a "good guy" or a "bad guy." He's not a costumed superhero devoting his life to fighting crime and stopping evil. Nor is he a villainous fiend intent on world domination or destruction.

At first, the Hulk appeared as a clever monster who plotted against his foes. Then Stan Lee and Jack Kirby decided to change his personality a bit. His brain power was lessened and the Hulk became a sad, lonely, persecuted figure, who simply wanted to be left alone.

He was more like an unhappy child, who couldn't understand why the world was always against him. This made him a more sympathetic character to readers of the Incredible Hulk comic book.

The Hulk was becoming a part of
Bruce Banner's personality. The
shy scientist, who had gone
through a difficult childhood, had
always controlled his anger. The
gamma rays that turned him into
the Hulk, released the angry side of
Banner's mind, turning him into a
raging green monster.

    The Hulk showed up whenever
Bruce Banner's
emotions got the
better of him.

In control
At first, Bruce
Banner's
change into the
Hulk was
triggered by
sunset. Then it
was set off by
anger. But for a
while, he could
control the
change simply
by thinking
about it!

Protective skin
Because
humans don't
have bullet-
resistant skin
like the Hulk,
they rely on
tanks with
thick metal
skin, bullet-
proof vests,
and helmets for
protection
while in battle.

Great strength
During times of
high stress or
anger, an
increase in
adrenaline
within his body
causes the
Hulk's strength
to increase
dramatically.

Powers of the Hulk

The Incredible Hulk has many
amazing powers. He is most famous
for his astounding strength. He can
lift about 100 tons with ease. Over
the years he has crushed cars, torn
trees from their roots, even split
open mountains. And, the madder
he gets, the stronger he gets!

His main form of travel is leaping. Although he doesn't actually fly, he can leap many miles in a single bound. When he lands, he creates craters in the earth.

The Hulk also heals at a very fast pace, allowing him to survive injuries that would kill even the hardiest human being.

Due to the gamma radiation within his body, fuelled by rage, the Hulk almost never gets tired. He can use his enormous strength and leaping ability for long periods of time. His enemies usually tire out long before he does!

His thick skin is resistant to most bullets, grenades, shells and rocket fire. His mind is also resistant to attacks from enemies with the ability to control the thoughts of others.

Let's face it—the Incredible Hulk is one really tough guy!

Strong men
Circuses and carnivals have always featured strong men, who lift huge amounts of weight.

Giant leaps!
Hulk's leaps can even take him up and out of the Earth's atmosphere!

Wedding bells
All was going well at the wedding of Bruce Banner and Betty Ross until Betty's father showed up. General Ross attempted to shoot Banner rather than let him marry his daughter. The bullet missed Banner, and the wedding went on!

Betty Ross

Dr. Bruce Banner has had his share of friends in both his human form and as the Incredible Hulk. The one person more special to him than all the others is Betty Ross, the daughter of the Hulk's biggest enemy, General "Thunderbolt" Ross.

Betty Ross was an only child. Her mother died when she was a teenager, and she always felt intimidated by her powerful father.

When Betty Ross met Bruce Banner, they instantly hit it off, and in no time at all they were very much in love.

They spoke of marriage despite the fact that General Ross was against their relationship because of his dislike of Banner.

At first, Betty didn't know that Bruce was also the Hulk. When she found out, their wedding plans were delayed. Banner was afraid of what he might do when he uncontrollably turned into the Hulk.

Eventually, when Bruce Banner and the Hulk were split into two separate beings, Bruce and Betty believed that the Hulk was out of their lives for good.

The wedding of Bruce Banner and Betty Ross finally took place in 1986. Soon after, however, Banner discovered that he could not live apart from the Hulk, and the two were merged once again. Betty had to deal with being married to both Banner and his big green counterpart.

Harpy
At one point Betty Ross transformed into a creature known as the Harpy. She had wings and could fire energy blasts from her hand.

Harpy eagle
The Harpy Eagle comes from South America. It has black and white feathers on its body and a gray head.

Rick Jones

Rick Jones was the teenage boy who was directly responsible for Bruce Banner becoming the Hulk.

Orphaned as an adolescent, Rick led a troubled life. When he was 16, another teenager dared him to drive his car out onto a restricted government facility. Rick took up the challenge and entered the test site of Banner's new gamma bomb.

Banner saw the teenager and managed to get him to safety before the bomb was detonated but was not so lucky himself. Banner was caught in the explosion that later caused him to transform into the Hulk.

Rick Jones felt he was responsible for Bruce Banner's condition and he soon became his best friend and protector. Rick needed to keep track of the Hulk and so he set up the Teen Brigade.

This was a group of young ham-radio enthusiasts who helped Rick Jones monitor the Hulk's activities. Rick was on hand during several key moments in the Hulk's life. He helped the Hulk escape from the army during his first encounter with the military. He also helped the Hulk battle against super-foes such as the Gargoyle, the Ringmaster, and Tyrannus. Rick almost made the ultimate sacrifice for his friend at Bruce's wedding. When General "Thunderbolt" Ross tried to shoot Bruce, the bullet hit Rick instead.

Captain America
Rick Jones wanted to be Captain America's sidekick. But the great hero refused to accept another young partner, because he had never gotten over the death of his original partner, Bucky.

Ham radio
Amateur or "ham" radio operators use their powerful radios to contact each other all around the world.

April Sommers
Unemployed model April Sommers helped Bruce through a tough time in his life, and the two became good friends.

Psychiatrists are doctors who study the workings of the human mind and help people with mental illnesses.

Doc Samson

Dr. Leonard Samson is a psychiatrist who is dedicated to finding a "cure" for Dr. Bruce Banner. He hopes to find a way of preventing him from changing into the Hulk, or to at least allow Bruce to have some control over his transformation.

When "Doc" Samson exposed himself to gamma radiation, he also underwent some changes. His hair turned green, his muscles grew huge, and he developed amazing super-human strength. As a psychiatrist, Samson is convinced that the Hulk represents the anger within Bruce and that dealing with this anger is the key to helping him.

Samson took on Banner's case and made it his personal mission to try and help the tortured scientist.

He created a special nutrient bath that physically separated Bruce Banner from the Hulk. At first, it appeared that the separation was a success and that Banner had finally been cured. Unfortunately, it soon became clear that, as separate beings, both Banner and the Hulk were growing weak. Neither could live without the other. When Samson realized this, the two were re-combined.

Doc Samson helped Bruce Banner to deal with his troubled childhood. Coming to grips with his past helped Banner to combine the three elements of his personality— the angry, slow-witted green Hulk, the intelligent and confident Gray Hulk, and meek, unhappy Bruce Banner.

Bereet
Bereet is an alien from the planet Krylor. She uses a device called the "Star Eye" to film beings from other planets, the Hulk included!

Film-making
On Earth, we don't have a "Star Eye." A movie is shot with a motion picture camera, and then projected onto a screen.

She-Hulk

Bruce Banner was visiting his cousin, Jennifer Walters. Jennifer, a defense attorney, was one of the few people who knew that Bruce was actually the Hulk.

When Jennifer was shot and needed blood, Bruce gave her an emergency transfusion of his own gamma-radiated blood. From that point on, when angered, Jennifer transformed into a 6-foot, 7-inch, 650-pound mountain of might who became known as She-Hulk.

There were many important differences between Jennifer Walters and her cousin. She could change into her powerful green form at will, and then change back again. She also retained her own personality when her body changed.

She-Hulk shared many of the Incredible Hulk's powers, such as super-human strength and leaping ability. Unlike her cousin, however, Jennifer had a great sense of humor. She really enjoyed transforming into a big green powerhouse. In fact, Jennifer actually *preferred* being in her She-Hulk form! She felt alive and free. It's lucky that she did, because Jennifer was exposed to an additional dose of gamma radiation that caused her to become the She-Hulk permanently.

Savage and Sensational
The "Sensational" She-Hulk from 1989 cracked jokes and even talked directly to her readers and to the writer of her comic (John Byrne). The original 1980 "Savage" version had more in common with her cranky cousin, the Incredible Hulk— including the shredded clothes!

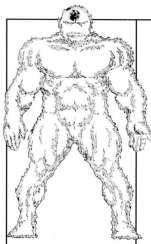

Zzzax
General Ross took part in an experiment to change himself into a super-human being by transferring some of the living electricity from a creature known as Zzzax into his own body. However, something went wrong, and Ross's mind was placed into the deadly Zzzax instead!

General Ross

The Hulk's most persistent foe is General Thaddeus E. "Thunderbolt" Ross. It was during World War II, he earned the nickname "Thunderbolt" because his troops thought that he struck like a bolt of thunder.

After serving in the Korean war, General Ross was assigned to Desert Base, in New Mexico, where he met Dr. Bruce Banner.

Ross immediately disliked Banner. Banner did not live up to what Ross thought a "real man" should be—tough and strong.

Following the explosion that transformed Banner into the Hulk, General Ross dedicated his life to finding and capturing the Green-Skinned Goliath—dead or alive! Ross eventually learned that Banner and the Hulk were one and the same.

The Pentagon put Ross in charge of "Operation Hulk," a U.S. military project that was set up to find, kill, or capture the Hulk, who was considered a menace. He assembled a team of operatives called "Hulkbusters" to help him track down the Emerald Behemoth.

In time, Ross's obsession with the Hulk and his hatred of Bruce Banner would drive the former military hero to madness.

Hulkbusters
Banner actually once led a team of Hulkbusters trying to track down the Green-Skinned Goliath.

The Pentagon
The Pentagon is a five-sided building that houses the U.S. military leaders. It was damaged in the terrorist attacks of September 11, 2001, but has since been rebuilt.

Madman
Samuel Sterns' brother Phil exposed himself to gamma radiation and became known as Madman. He has amazing strength, the ability to increase and decrease his mass, and also to change his shape and form. He has a great knowledge of gamma radiation, having been a classmate of Bruce Banner's.

The Leader

Samuel Sterns was working in a government-owned chemical research facility in the Nevada desert. His job was to transport cylinders filled with radioactive waste. In a freak accident, one of the cylinders exploded, and Sterns was exposed to huge amounts of dangerous gamma radiation.

Although he was not injured in the explosion, several days later Sterns' brain and head grew unusually large, and just like the Hulk, his skin turned bright green. Sterns found that he could read at an incredibly fast pace, and his overall intelligence had reached superhuman levels! Just as gamma radiation had transformed Bruce Banner's body, it changed Samuel Sterns' brain.

Unfortunately, Sterns decided to use his newfound intelligence for crime. He set up an international crime syndicate and adopted the name "The Leader." He soon tired of relying on criminals with less intellect than himself, and so he disbanded the group.

The Leader built robots called humanoids and began working as a lone criminal mastermind. His aim was to conquer the world. The Hulk has stopped the Leader's many attempts at global domination.

The Bi-Beast
Bi-Beast was created by a race of bird-like aliens to keep their cultural history and their skills in warfare from fading away.

Robots
Although once the realm of science fiction, today robots can do everything from mowing the lawn or building a car, to performing dangerous scientific experiments.

Tyrannus
Tyrannus is an immortal being who discovered a fountain of youth beneath the Earth's surface. When he attacked U.S. armed forces, General Ross called in the Hulk to stop him.

The Abomination

One of the Hulk's toughest foes is the Abomination. A spy named Emil Blonsky was exposed to a gamma-radiation burst of even higher power than the one that turned Bruce Banner into the Hulk. In fact, this exposure took place in Bruce Banner's lab.

Blonsky had the same genetic factor in his body that Bruce Banner had, preventing him from being killed by high levels of gamma radiation. Like Banner, Blonsky, also transformed into a huge, monstrous creature.

This powerful, strange being was named the Abomination by General Ross.

The Abomination had even greater strength than the Hulk. In their first battle, the Abomination defeated the Hulk. He then kidnapped Betty Ross.

General Ross, the Hulk's longtime enemy was forced to ask the Hulk for help in rescuing Betty. As Bruce Banner, he developed a gamma device which lowered the Abomination's power, making it equal to that of the Hulk's. This allowed the Emerald Behemoth to finally defeat his powerful foe.

Rhino
Rhino is protected by a super-tough suit that simulates the hide of a real rhinoceros. Rhino teamed up with the Abomination to take on the Hulk.

The Abomination, one of the few creatures in the Marvel Universe with more strength than the Incredible Hulk!

Wolverine, the X-Man

Wolverine is a member of the mutant group, the X-Men. He has claws made from an unbreakable metal called adamantium, and is a fierce fighter with extraordinary healing ability.

Wendigo

Wendigo was the strongest foe the Hulk ever fought. The Wendigo is a creature that was once a human being but has been magically transformed into a huge beast.

As time passed, the human's mind faded away, replaced by that of a ferocious animal.

The Wendigo stands ten feet tall and is covered with white fur. Residing in the Canadian North Woods, Wendigo has super-human strength equal to that of the Hulk's.

The Wendigo also has a great resistance to pain and injury. It is practically impossible to kill this creature! It has withstood powerful blows from the Hulk and severe wounds from Wolverine's claws, and survived both.

In their first battle, Hulk was surprised to take on a creature with strength equal to his own. Wendigo won that contest. Later, the Hulk returned to the Canadian North Woods where he and Wolverine teamed up to defeat the powerful creature.

Wolverine, the animal
A real-life wolverine is the largest member of the weasel family. It is a heavy, short-legged animal, that looks a bit like a small bear. Its tail is bushy and its paws are large, with sharp claws. It's extremely strong and is a fierce fighter.

WHAT A STROKE OF LUCK! ALL I HAVE TO DO IS KEEP MY FINGER OFF THE "HOLD" BUTTON, AND IT'LL BE THE END OF BRUCE BANNER!

Igor Starsky
Soviet spy Igor Starsky desperately tried to learn the secret of Bruce Banner's gamma bomb. But Banner refused to share his scientific knowledge with anyone. When Banner ran into the desert testing site, Starsky failed to stop the bomb from exploding. He was later killed by the Hulk.

Gargoyle

The man who came to be known as the Gargoyle was a scientist working for the Soviet Union during the Cold War. He was forced by the Soviet government to take part in dangerous atomic tests. During one of these tests, an accident took place that unleashed powerful radiation. The radiation altered his face and body. His head grew large and misshapen. That's how he earned the cruel nickname, Gargoyle.

This accident also greatly increased the Gargoyle's intelligence level. He was now a genius and the most brilliant scientist in the Soviet Union. The Soviets put him to work as a master spy.

The Gargoyle sent one of his agents, a man named Igor Starsky, to spy on Dr. Bruce Banner's development of the gamma bomb. It was Starsky who failed to stop the countdown for the testing of the gamma bomb that resulted in Bruce Banner becoming the Hulk. The Gargoyle wanted to be a normal human being again, even though it meant sacrificing his newfound intelligence. Bruce Banner agreed to help him by creating a radiation device that changed the Gargoyle back into a human.

Gargoyles
Gargoyles are usually found as decorative elements on buildings. They take the form of animals or fantastic creatures.

Absorbing Man
This enemy can change his body into anything he touches, including steel, stone, wood, fire, or water!

Captain America
A true American hero, Captain America was created during World War II as a super soldier. Frozen in suspended animation after the war, he awoke in the 1960s, and still continues to battle evil while searching for his place in a changing world.

The Avengers

The Avengers was Marvel's first superhero team. The group's original five members were the Hulk, Iron Man, Thor, Ant-Man, and Wasp. Over the years, many of Marvel's greatest heroes joined the Avengers. The roster of members changed on a regular basis.

The original group came together when the Hulk was framed for a train wreck that injured many people. Rick Jones didn't believe that the Hulk would intentionally hurt innocent people. He sent out a radio message to the Fantastic Four asking for their help.

Instead, the message was received by Thor, Ant-Man, Iron Man, and the Wasp. Together these four heroes found the Hulk. Working as a team, they proved the Hulk's innocence.

Ant-Man suggested that the five form a regular team. They agreed.

Always a loner by nature, the Hulk left the Avengers only a few weeks after the group was formed. He was replaced by Captain America.

The Avengers' mansion
The Avengers' mansion is three stories high and has a basement plus two sub-basement levels. The building contains a landing runway for the Avengers' supersonic jets, a combat simulation room, a full gym, and an arcade game room.

The Avengers first lineup comprised clockwise from left: Thor, Iron Man, Ant-Man, the Wasp, and the Hulk.

The Defenders

What do you get when you take three loners, three brooding misfits who have always preferred to work by themselves, and put them together into a superhero team? You get the Defenders, the greatest "non-team" to ever work together against evil.

Silver Surfer
The first superhero to join the Defenders after the original three members was the Silver Surfer. This humanoid alien, named Norrin Radd rides through the cosmos on his long silver surfboard, selflessly protecting both his own people and the people of Earth.

In 1972, the Hulk, Prince Namor the Sub-Mariner, and Doctor Strange, Master of the Mystic Arts, joined forces (kind of) and became the Defenders.

Surf's up!
Surfing is an ancient sport that grew to great popularity in Hawaii in the 1920s. The late 1950s saw an explosion of surfing, along with surf music, movies, and fashion, mostly in California.

Namor is the son of Princess Fen of the undersea kingdom called Atlantis and an American naval officer. He is strong, and can move through water at 60 miles per hour.

Doctor Stephen Strange, a brilliant neurosurgeon, journeyed to the Himalayan Mountains. There he met the Ancient One, a sorcerer, who taught him the ways of the Mystic Arts. Dr. Strange can hypnotize people, hurl magical bolts, and project his spirit through time and space.

Unlike the Avengers, the Defenders had no official charter or rules to govern them. They had no permanent headquarters, and no set roster of members.

Himalayas
The Himalayan Mountains run along 1,500 miles in Asia. This snow-covered range rises to nearly 30,000 feet.

Hulk vs. Thing

The Fantastic Four
Marvel's first superhero team consisted of Reed Richards who became Mister Fantastic—he has the ability to stretch his body to great lengths; Sue Storm, his wife, who became Invisible Girl; Johnny Storm, her brother, who became the Human Torch; and Ben Grimm who became the Thing.

Who's stronger, the Incredible Hulk or the Thing?

This question has been debated among Marvel readers since both incredibly powerful characters burst onto the comic book scene in the early 1960s.

The Thing, whose real name is Ben Grimm, is a member of the Fantastic Four, the superhero team that launched the Marvel Age of comics in 1961. Along with the other members of the team, Ben was exposed to cosmic radiation while piloting a space ship. Just as gamma radiation changed Bruce Banner into the Hulk, this cosmic energy transformed Ben Grimm into the Thing.

When Grimm first became the Thing, his strength was no match for the Hulk's. As the years went on, the Thing's strength grew.

Like his big green counterpart, the Thing gets stronger when he gets mad. Often a battle between Hulk and Thing hinges on the emotions of the two rather than simply physical strength or combat skill. Neither is evil, and both behemoths have been greatly misunderstood. So who's stronger? That question may never definitively be answered.

Ben Grimm
Ben Grimm had a troubled childhood. He belonged to a gang. His aunt and uncle helped straighten him out, and he eventually graduated from college and joined the U.S. Air Force.

Alicia Masters
After Ben Grimm became the Thing, he was always angry, until he met Alicia Masters, a blind sculptress who loved him without judgment.

Hulk vs. Hulk?

In 1991, in issue #377 of *The Incredible Hulk*, comic book history was made. This groundbreaking tale, written by Peter David, featured a battle between the green Hulk and the gray Hulk. The green Hulk was angry, childlike, of low intelligence. The gray Hulk had much of Bruce Banner's intellect, but showed little of Banner's kindness.

Over the years, there were times when Banner had Hulk's body and his own mind. In his attempts to "cure" Banner, Doc Samson managed to separate the Green Hulk from Bruce Banner. He even brought back the gray Hulk, not seen since the very first issue in 1962.

But when issue #377 hit the stands, Bruce Banner, green Hulk, and gray Hulk were all sitting together in Doc Samson's office.

Evolution
At first the Hulk was just an angry creature. Over time he was presented as a living version of Bruce Banner's anger.

The Professor
Following "session" with Doc Samson, the three parts of the Hulk were united, a combination known as the Professor.

How was this possible?

As the amazing story unfolded, readers came to realize that the three parts of Bruce Banner only co-existed in his mind. As a psychiatrist, Doc Samson was able to put all three parts of Banner's mind back together in an effort to heal him.

And so, the story goes on, and another generation is thrilled by new tales of the Incredible Hulk.

Landmark
The cover to the classic *Incredible Hulk #377.*

Glossary

Astounding
Amazing, unbelievable.

Behemoth
A huge creature.

Binoculars
A device that allows a person to use both eyes at once to view distant objects.

Brutish
Behaving like a beast.

Counterpart
A partner, or someone that is strongly connected to an individual.

Devious
Crooked, planning and scheming to deceive.

Disoriented
Confused, unsure.

Frail
Delicate, fragile.

Groundbreaking
Innovative, brand new, never been done before.

Harness
To capture and control.

Infiltrate
To get inside secretly.

Intention
Purpose, plan, moving toward a goal.

Merge
Blend together.

Neurosurgeon
A doctor who operates on the nervous system, including the brain and the spinal cord.

Nickname
A substitute name given to a person, place, or thing.

Nucleus
The central part of an atom, containing protons and neutrons.

Operatives
Agents, those who work for an organization.

Perished
Died, destroyed.

Persecute
To oppress or harass.

Persistent
Staying stubbornly committed to a goal.

Radiation
Energy sent out as atoms and molecules go through internal changes.

Rampaging
To rush about violently.

Restricted
Prevented from access.

Science fiction
Fantastic stories involving imagined scientific phenomenon.

Scientist
A person who studies and works with some branch of science.

Selfless
Having more regard for someone else's interests than your own.

Simulation
A representation of something that is not the actual object or experience.

Spy
An agent who gathers information about another country.

Terrain
A portion of land, usually referring to its physical features.

Transformation
Change.

Uncontrolled
Wild, unstoppable.

Withdrawn
Shy.

Index